# WITH NO STRINGS ATTACHED

## 28 Days of Blessing Your Wife

STEVEN H. BELL D.MIN.

Bell Brother's Press
Hope for Families

*To Meredith,*
*You are an amazing wife, mother, and woman.*
*I am blessed beyond words to not only have you in my life,*
*but to be married to you.*


*To the people called White's Chapel,*
*My family and I are privileged to be a part of such a tremendous community of*
*faith.*
*I am grateful to our Co-Pastors, Dr. John McKellar and Dr. Todd Renner,*
*for your consistently competent and effective leadership.*
*I am inspired by the amazing WC|MEN*
*who unconditionally love and reveal Jesus Christ in this world.*
*Thank you, Dr Harville Hendrix, for putting me on the path,*
*Cathy Watson, for your diligent proofreading of this manuscript,*
*Doug Kovach, for your keen eye with photography,*
*and Dr. Larry Duggins, for your guidance with this project.*
*You all are a great blessing to me!*

# TABLE OF CONTENTS

# PREFACE

*"Therefore shall a man leave his father and his mother, and shall cleave unto his wife: and they shall be one flesh"* (Genesis 2:24).

"Quoted throughout the Bible, this verse gives us the foundational charge about what it is to be a husband... but what does it mean for us to "cleave" to our wives? What does unwavering support and courageous loyalty look like – and, maybe more importantly – how do we live this verse into reality?

In our world of inch-deep and mile-wide relationships, there is nothing more important (and no greater blessing) in our lives than strong marriages. Dr. Steven Bell has written a delightful and insightful twenty-eight day guide that will help us focus on how to keep our marriages fresh and alive.

This book will guide us to a deeper appreciation of and respect for our wives, for the women and companions that God created them to be. Out of this renewed awareness, true love deepens and grows, and we find ourselves more in love as we find ourselves more in service. This book, also, provides practical and helpful ways to maintain true and mutually fulfilling intimacy.

As humorous as it is honest, these reflections give down-to-earth tips to keep marriage partners from taking each other for granted. At the heart of it, Dr. Bell dispels the myths of sacrifice-free love to get to the truth of abiding love as he explores the spiritual component of marriage... knowing that it is only a life and marriage grounded in Christ that unites us into "one flesh."

We can't think of any marriage that will not be blessed and encouraged by the sage advice that Dr. Bell offers."

Dr. John McKellar & Dr. Todd Renner
Co-Pastors, White's Chapel United Methodist Church

"This is a book for men who want a happy marriage written by a man who knows the secret!! It's simple! Be a source of blessings to her! Steven Bell has distilled the essential ingredients of blessings and put them on a daily schedule, so there is nothing to do but do them. I recommend this book to all men, and I encourage all wives to get it and give it to their husbands."

Harville Hendrix, Ph. D.
Co-author with Helen LaKelly Hunt of *Making Marriage Simple*

# INTRODUCTION

Marriage is one of the most exciting, frustrating, life-giving, confusing, reward-ing, draining, and worthwhile relationships known to humankind. In fact, President Abraham Lincoln once commented, "Marriage is neither heaven nor hell, it is simply purgatory." At a time when the average age of people getting married is going up (not to mention the divorce and cohabitation rate), marriage needs a makeover (and so does love!). We need a new view and vision for this holy covenant that exists between a man and a woman.

"With no strings attached" is urban slang for entering into a relationship (usu-ally sexual in nature) with a very low level of commitment. Unfortunately, mar-riage has succumbed to the fleeting whims of our contemporary culture. Ours is a culture that values entitlement over hard work, happiness over faithfulness, constant indulgence over moderation, self-gratification over selfless service, and quick fixes over resolve. Ours is a culture that rarely contemplates the long-term consequences that come with wanting things our way right away as opposed to wanting what's best for the greater good in God's time. I love the picture I came across a few months ago that depicted an elderly married couple sitting next to each other, the caption stating, "A reporter asked the couple, 'How did you man-age to stay together for 65 years?' The woman replied, 'We were born in a time when if something was broken we would fix it, not throw it away...'" My friend, we live not in that time. And something must change. In the following pages I'm going to give you a different take on the phrase, "with no strings attached."

So whether you are married (which is the primary relationship dynamic I'll be focusing on in this book), engaged, dating, or praying for a woman who will just say "Yes" to grabbin' some coffee with you, buddy, you need to read this. I'll never forget what my dog Blue used to do. Blue was a Blue-Healer/Rottweiler mix, and Blue loved poo (yes, I couldn't even get through the introduction without potty talk coming out!). My mother-in-law is a rancher, and when I would take Blue out to her land, Blue would jump out of the bed of my 3/4-ton 4X4 GMC Sierra (yes, I'm a manly man who drives a truck), run as fast as she could to the nearest freshest pile of fly-covered cow manure, and then roll in it until she looked like the Creature from Boggy Creek. She would then sprint back to me, take a seat right at my feet, wag her tail, grin, and share all that she had experienced with me (thank God I don't have a sense of smell!). So maybe I'm pushing the envelope with this illustration just a tad, but that is exactly what I think you need to do with this book. You need to read it, digest it, roll around in it, play with it, savor it, let God do some great things in your marriage through you, and then share what you've learned with somebody.

The theme of the following pages is all about blessing that special woman in your life. We see a curious thing happen in Genesis 12:2. God says to Abram, "I will make of you a great nation and will bless you. I will make your name respected, and you will be a blessing" (CEB). Men, we are so very and incredibly blessed by God. And what I'm asking you to do isn't all that radical or original, but it will be challenging. I'm asking you to bless your wife with no strings attached. Behave toward her in ways that bless or increase her physical, intellectual, emotional, social, and spiritual health. I don't come to you as an expert in this subject matter, but rather as someone who has a lot of rough edges and a lot to learn. However, this I have come to believe: Whether you know it or not, whether you treat her so or not, that woman whose ring you wear is the most important human being in your life. Your marriage constitutes the most important human relationship in your life. It's time to acknowledge that. It's time to get to work. It's time to focus on your wife, with no strings attached.

# BLESS HER SELF

*"Everything has beauty, but not everyone sees it"* (Confucius).

What I'm going to share with you in the following pages is really more of a "how to" on blessing your wife, much of which comes from my own personal experience as a husband and a pastor. However, if you are interested in a more thorough treatment of the deep, dark, mysterious reasons for doing such a thing, then I encourage you to pick up a copy of *For Men Only* by Shaunti and Jeff Feldhahn.[1] I find their research to be quite helpful in answering the question, "Why?"

For the first week of this journey we're going to talk about blessing your wife just as she is – her physical self. We're going to look at the way you talk to her, touch her, connect with her, and appreciate her. We're going to dabble in exercise and nutrition (and I mean dabble!). And we're even going to hit sex (if we're getting to sex in week one, I bet you can't wait for weeks two through four!). But the whole point of this is that you behave toward your wife in a way that makes her feel beautiful, because she is beautiful. And whether you know it or not, you have the power to make her feel that way. You also have the power to make her feel ugly

---

1  Feldhahn, Shaunti and Jeff. *For Men Only, Revised and Updated Edition: A Straightforward Guide to the Inner Lives of Women* (Colorado Springs: Multnomah Books, 2013).

and inadequate. Now, you're a smart man, and you know which outcome you want for your wife. So I hope you choose wisely, consistently.

I'll never forget one of the first times I cooked dinner for my wife, Meredith. She'll be coming up a lot in the following pages. I became a pastor for the first time (thank you Pecan Gap and Ladonia United Methodist Churches - you were so wonderful to a green pastor!) in June of 1999. I met Meredith on August 28 of that same year. I was a second-year seminary student at Perkins School of Theology at Southern Methodist University in Dallas, TX, that August, and she was a first-year student there (having recently graduated from Texas A&M University in College Station). We became engaged in December of that same year, with plans to be married the following July 2000. Yes, when we got married we had not even known each other for a full year – scary! So there we were in the Pecan Gap parsonage. It was sometime during the Spring of 2000. We were both full-time students. I was the pastor of two small rural congregations. Meredith was on the student ministry staff of First United Methodist Church of Dallas. We had two dogs, two sets of bills (because Meredith had her own place in Dallas, of course), no money, and not enough time to spend together. Oh yeah, and there was this little thing called a wedding that was coming up, quickly! She had driven out to see me on a Saturday (about an hour-and-15-minute drive from Dallas), and I cooked her dinner. I must say, the pasta was overcooked, the sauce needed to be warmed up a little bit, and I can't remember if I actually cooked meatballs or not; but I called it "spaghetti." And when we sat down to eat, big tears began rolling down her cheeks. Of course I became incredibly self-conscious about having done something wrong (because I had done a number of things wrong – and some things never change), but she stopped those incorrect thoughts by simply saying, "Those are grateful tears." That moment became a holy one for me. With just a little effort, I had done something (with no strings attached) for my fiancée that blessed her.

Hopefully the next seven days will give you some fuel to do the same for your wife. God bless you, now go bless your wife!

# DAY 1 - SPEAK KIND WORDS

*"Death and life are in the power of the tongue..."* (Proverbs 18:21 CEB).

*"Kind words can be short and easy to speak but their echoes are truly endless"* (Mother Teresa).

## Thought for the Day:

I was headed toward Louisiana late one night when I stopped at an East Texas gas station to grab a burger and use the restroom. Above the urinal I noticed a plaque that referenced a historical conversation between Nancy Astor (the first female member of the House of Commons in Britain) and Winston Churchill. The two obviously had some animosity between them. In fact, it was so great that when Churchill was at the Astor mansion, a hostile Lady Astor said to him (while coffee was being served), "Winston, if I were your wife, I'd put poison in your coffee." To that Churchill replied, "Nancy, if I were your husband, I'd drink it." Is this exchange a picture of your marriage? Do you speak similar words to your wife (or think them)?

The tongue has been likened to the small rudder that controls a large ship, the tiny metal bit that controls a much larger horse, and a single match that can create a huge forest fire (James 3). Truly, as Proverbs teaches us, "death and life are in the power of the tongue." How do you speak to your wife? Are you always nagging (that's not just something that wives do!), complaining, and criticizing? If you were to ask your wife whether or not you speak kind words to her, how would she answer? When would the last time be that she could recall you speaking kind words to her? You want to be a person who gives life to your wife, not someone who sucks it out of her. And the tongue is one of the primary tools utilized in giving your wife life or death.

When I get stressed or tired, I get negative. And unfortunately, my family feels the effects of that stress. It's really an area of growth for me. I'll never forget the time when I had a long run of stress in the office. I cannot remember what it was that was stressing me out so much, but every day I would come home, walk through the back door, and as Meredith would ask me how my day went I would just start complaining. It was a habit in which I was stuck. It started about stuff going on concerning other people, but it would oftentimes change direction towards her. I was a selfish dark cloud with nothing positive or life-giving to say to anyone, especially my wife (which is a fancy way of saying that I was totally taking her for granted). Thank goodness, one day Meredith had had enough. I came in the door, and just as I began my routine gripe session she stopped me cold. She told me, "Steven, from now on when you walk through that door, you are going to say, 'Today was the best day of my life. I am so happy. It was just a wonderful day!'" And being the smart man that I am, I followed her lead. I did that very thing. I would come in the house from my crummy day, and lie. I would exclaim how great of a day I'd had and how marvelous it had been. The funny thing is, the more I spoke those words in jest to my wife each day, the better I started feeling about my days. Life got better. I felt happy, and joy was mine. It's because I was not only speaking words of life to Meredith, but also to myself. It changed me. It can change you as well.

Ephesians 4:29 states, "Don't let any foul words come out of your mouth. Only say what is helpful when it is needed for building up the community so that it benefits those who hear what you say" (CEB). Apply Paul's words to your wife, and you will bless her.

---

### Task to Consider:

Compliment your wife's appearance daily.

---

# DAY 2 - THE POWER OF A TOUCH

*"Jesus went home with Peter and saw Peter's mother-in-law lying in bed with a fever. He touched her hand, and the fever left her. Then she got up and served them"* (Matthew 8:14, 15 CEB).

*"I've learned that every day you should reach out and touch someone. People love a warm hug, or just a friendly pat on the back"* (Maya Angelou).

## Thought for the Day:

I just love this passage from the Gospel of Matthew. Jesus goes to Peter's home, and there he finds Peter's mother-in-law sick. And of course Jesus does what he does so well, he heals. His healing power flows into her and she recovers. The disease in her body is cured. The life that she loves returns to her. And how does this happen? Through the power of a touch. Now, I've often wondered what Peter thought about Jesus healing his mother-in-law. He might have been hoping that she would just kick the bucket, and possibly could have been a little ticked off at Jesus for demonstrating such compassion and love. But I doubt it. I know you would never think that about your mother-in-law!

And did you notice what happened after Jesus touched her? The first thing that happened was she got up. This is a picture of resurrection, death to life. She snapped to. Something tremendously good had happened to her, and you can't keep a good woman down. The second thing that happened was that she began serving her guests. She engaged in ministry. The gratitude she had for the healing power that had filled her body naturally overflowed to the rest of the folks in her home.

You, my friend, have a very similar power. To come into contact with your wife (and I don't mean elbowing her out of the way as you race off to the latest Cabela's

sale!) creates a sense of intimacy between the two of you, it makes her feel secure, and (as Maya Angelou alludes to) it just feels nice. A good rule of thumb
is that if your wife comes into your presence (or if you are just generally around
each other), touch her (and I don't just mean in the bedroom – try the kitchen,
laundry room, closet, or wherever you happen to find each other). Now, please, I
said touch her, don't grope her. Can I say that? Tenderly (not a guy word) place a
hand on her shoulder. Give her a hug. Kiss her cheek or neck. Hold her hand. But
remember, there are NO STRINGS ATTACHED to this blessing. If you do this
with high hopes of ending up in the bedroom, then your motivation is less than
pure. Your single motive should be to bless her, nothing more, nothing less. That
back massage serves as a way to let her know that you appreciate her and want to
help ease some of her stress, period.

I know you've probably heard enough by now, and are ready to  graciously donate
this book to a local charity for a small tax write-off (or delete is off your wireless
device), but I dare you to keep reading. I triple-dog dare you. Who can resist that!

---

### Task to Consider:

Hold your wife's hand, or even better, give her a hug for one full minute.

---

# DAY 3 - CONNECTION IS CRITICAL

*"Don't stop meeting together with other believers, which some people have gotten into the habit of doing. Instead, encourage each other, especially as you see the day drawing near"* (Hebrews 10:25 CEB).

*"Love is our true destiny. We do not find the meaning of life by ourselves alone - we find it with another"* (Thomas Merton).

## Thought for the Day:

Meredith and I are about to celebrate 13 years of marriage. Pretty amazing if you ask me! However, a few years ago we found ourselves sitting in a counselor's office. There was no affair, no abuse, no addiction, no crisis. The truth is, there wasn't much of anything but a commitment to each other and 2 beautiful children. Our marriage had become stale, for both of us. I'm thankful for that counselor (and to the counseling profession in general) because she helped us to diagnose the problem. We had simply lost our connection with each other. We had become great business partners with benefits. Life was about work, kids, stuff, and food. And what's so alarming for me is that I know countless couples who are right where we were.

That's right, I said "where we were," because we are not there now. And if that's not good enough news, then I'll give you some more. It took very little time, effort, or energy to get out of our slump. Here's what we did. We figured out how to speak love to each other.[2] Meredith loves to give presents to people (it's one of her spiritual gifts), and so she would give me presents all the time to show her love for me. The problem is, receiving gifts doesn't make me feel loved. What makes me

---

2  For more information, check out www.5lovelanguages.com/profile/.

feel loved is when someone says something nice about me or touches me. I wasn't doing a very good job of speaking love to Meredith either. So we figured it out, and got to work loving each other.

The second thing we started doing was to intentionally spend time together. We would set aside 20 minutes a day to sit down on the couch, put all media away (phones, TV, iPad, etc.), look into each other's eyes, and talk. Now, we wouldn't talk about the kids, or work, or the normal husband-and-wife mumblings. We would (and still do) talk about our hopes and dreams together as husband and wife. That time became critically meaningful to us, slowing us down from our hurried pace, and allowing for some much-needed connection to bind us together again.

Maintaining connection with your wife is especially critical when you are in a state of conflict with one another. At these times men naturally retreat, withdraw, shut down, or go silent, but what your wife needs from you is to know that connection has not been severed. Work it out. Talk it through. Let her know you are angry, but that you also still love her. And stay connected with her.

Check out Hebrews 10:25 (above), apply it to your marriage, and your wife will experience blessing (and so will you!).

---

### Task to Consider:

Stop, sit, and speak with your wife.

---

# DAY 4 - PUT HER BEFORE YOU

*"Don't do anything for selfish purposes, but with humility think of others as better than yourselves. Instead of each person watching out for their own good, watch out for what is better for others"* (Philippians 2:3, 4 CEB).

*"Above all the grace and the gifts that Christ gives to his beloved is that of overcoming self"* (St. Francis of Assisi).

## Thought for the Day:

One of the greatest challenges all human beings face (repeatedly) is the fight against narcissism. We fight against our predisposition to be first, to be right (all the time), and to be God. We would gladly take our place at the center of the universe and let everything (and everyone) revolve around us (and we oftentimes think that's exactly what's going on). But that is just not reality. People who exalt themselves get humbled (check out Matthew 23:11 and 12), sooner or later. Time, experience, relationships, and hard knocks (otherwise known as pain and suffering) teach us that the universe does not revolve around us, we are not in the driver's seat, and that there truly is a God (and it is not you or me). So our trajectory for life is to learn to put God first, and to put others before ourselves. Jesus tells us that the greatest activity is to love God and to love others (Matthew 22), and Paul tells us that love is not self-seeking (1 Corinthians 13:5).

Jesus tells us, "No one has greater love than to give up one's life for one's friends" (John 15:13 CEB). And what's so amazingly interesting is that he not only tells us to do this, he actually does it. He practices what he preaches. After Paul gives us these words on selflessness from Philippians 2:3 and 4, he goes right into an illustration of that wisdom. And of course his illustration is Jesus. Jesus, who humbled himself by journeying from Heaven to Earth, put on flesh, and was born of the Virgin Mary. Jesus, who emptied himself by submitting himself to a horrible death by crucifixion. That's our model, guys. Follow well.

And of course the Number One person that you need to practice such behavior with is your wife. Serve your wife. Sacrifice for your wife. Stretch for your wife. We get so caught up in thinking that our wives are supposed to be servile and submissive to us, that we forget what Ephesians 5:21 states. Paul writes, "and submit to each other out of respect for Christ" (CEB). Yes, he says, "submit to each other." Marriage is about mutuality and mutual submission. It's a reciprocal relationship between two equal parties. It's a holy covenant not to be entered into leisurely or lightly (because it will change you). Marriage is not about power or control. If there is a hierarchy in your marriage, then it's not much of a marriage (and it's far from God's design for marriage). If you think you are better than or have more say in your marriage than your wife, then you need a reality check. And I think you need to start reading the Bible! Put her before you. Lay aside your selfish ambitions and pride (otherwise known as sin). And humble yourself. Just try it. Your wife will be blessed, and so will your marriage.

---

### Task to Consider:

Open the door for your wife.

---

# DAY 5 - EXERCISE FOR QUALITY OF LIFE

*"Or don't you know that your body is a temple of the Holy Spirit who is in you? Don't you know that you have the Holy Spirit from God, and you don't belong to yourselves? You have been bought and paid for, so honor God with your body"* (1 Corinthians 6:19, 20 CEB).

*"Leave all the afternoon for exercise and recreation, which are as necessary as reading. I will rather say more necessary because health is worth more than learning"* (Thomas Jefferson).

## Thought for the Day:

Now, let me be very clear. I am no exercise or physical education guru. I am a pastor, which usually means I eat way too much and don't get enough exercise. However, I am a runner, and have learned the value of exercise. Let me ask you this question: Why do you exercise (if indeed you do)? To look good? To feel good? I'd say those are decent answers, and definitely normal. But I think there is something more to all of this exercise stuff.

You can go to the gym, or strap on your running shoes, so you can keep up that nice hunky figure. You can engage in physical conditioning so when people look at you they think, "Wow, he's fit." You can get your time in on the elliptical machine so when you look in the mirror you don't scream (or wonder who that person is). Or your motivation can be very different. The truth is, you want to bless your wife and family. And one way to bless them is to be there for them as long as possible. So my encouragement to you today is to work out, sweat, and engage in physical activity so you can be healthy and live a good long life for them. It really has little to do with your physical appearance. It has everything to do with blessing longevity. She needs you. She always will.

There is another reason to get or stay in shape. It has to do with the passage from 1 Corinthians 6 (above). Although that passage is specifically talking about avoiding sexual immorality, I would like to think that it applies here. We honor God with our bodies because our body is the temple of the Holy Spirit. God's Spirit is in each of us, housed in this vessel of flesh and blood. I love the Easter story from the Gospel of John. John writes, "Early in the morning of the first day of the week, while it was still dark, Mary Magdalene came to the tomb and saw that the stone had been taken away from the tomb. She ran to Simon Peter and the other disciple, the one whom Jesus loved, and said, 'They have taken the Lord from the tomb, and we don't know where they've put him.' Peter and the other disciple left to go to the tomb. They were running together, but the other disciple ran faster than Peter and was the first to arrive at the tomb" (John 20:1-4 CEB). Mary ran. Peter ran. John ran (and he won!). They all ran, to Jesus. Jesus had risen from the dead. He was alive. The world would never be the same again. So run, exercise, and sweat; but do it as a means to honor God with your body. Do it as a way to seek and share Jesus (because you can't minister in his name if you're dead!). Do it in order to protect this house that shelters God's Holy Spirit within you.

---

### *Task to Consider:*

Take a walk with your wife.

---

# DAY 6 - KNOW WHEN TO SAY WHEN

*"Don't hang out with those who get drunk on wine or those who eat too much meat"*
(Proverbs 23:20 CEB).

*"If we could give every individual the right amount of nourishment and exercise,*
*not too little and not too much, we would have found the safest way to health"*
(Hippocrates).

## Thought for the Day:

OK, so nutrition is another area where I know I fall short. My diet doesn't begin
to include enough veggies. I consume way too many QT Freezonis, eat way too
much fried chicken, and drink my weight in coffee. I've recently cut out most
sweets from my diet (we'll see how long that lasts!), and that is definitely a step in
the right direction, but boy do I have a long way to go. However, the issue I want
to talk about today goes far beyond healthy eating, I want to talk about gluttony
(no, anything but that!). Billy Graham has said, "Gluttony is a sin that most of us
commit, but few of us mention. It is one of the prevalent sins among Christians."

Do you have trouble knowing when to say when (and I don't just mean in your
alcohol consumption)? Is "enough" a word in your vocabulary? Do you try to eat,
drink, or consume your troubles away, only to find that your dissatisfaction with
life persists? If so, then you, my friend, could possibly have an issue with gluttony.
And it is going to be hard to bless your wife when all you are personally focused
on is "more."

Paul writes, "As I have told you many times and now say with deep sadness, many
people live as enemies of the cross. Their lives end with destruction. Their god is
their stomach, and they take pride in their disgrace because their thoughts focus

on earthly things. Our citizenship is in heaven. We look forward to a savior that comes from there – the Lord Jesus Christ. He will transform our humble bodies so that they are like his glorious body, by the power that also makes him able to subject all things to himself" (Philippians 3:18-21 CEB). I know you just read that, but please take a moment and read it again. Do you see what Paul is saying? There is only one true answer to our craving. No amount of food, drink, sex, gadgets, titles, or sporting goods will satisfy. In fact, Paul goes as far as to say that if you are living to satisfy your earthly desires with earthly substances, then you are an "enemy of the cross." I don't think any of us want that.

So what do we do? Jesus tells us. He says, "I am the bread of life. Whoever comes to me will never go hungry, and whoever believes in me will never be thirsty" (John 6:35 CEB). You can attempt to satisfy your hunger with the things of this world, and your stomach will still growl (along with your soul). Or you can seek a personal relationship with God through Jesus Christ. I know it's easy for me to say this, but it will take you your entire life to perfect it (but guys like challenges, right?). If you want real joy, peace, and satisfaction; then go get it. And don't forget to share this Bread with your wife, because He is the biggest blessing.

---

### Task to Consider:

Make dinner for your wife.

---

# DAY 7 - INTIMACY DOESN'T MEAN SEX

*"This is the reason that a man leaves his father and mother and embraces his wife, and they become one flesh. The two of them were naked, the man and his wife, but they weren't embarrassed"* (Genesis 2:24, 25 CEB).

*"It's not economical to go to bed early to save the candles if the result is twins"* (Chinese Proverb).

## Thought for the Day:

Good news – your wife has a serious need for intimacy that must be met (of course by you!). Bad news – that doesn't mean sex. OK, so if you're married, then chances are you've had some frustration with your wife over the frequency of your sexual activities. If it was up to you, the two of you would have sex at least twice a day (every day). But with your wife, it normally will be much less. However, since this collection is not so much about you as it is focused on helping you to bless your wife with no strings attached – let's talk about her. Not what you want her to do for you. Not what you even need. But what she needs from you.

Barbara Cartland states, "Among men, sex sometimes results in intimacy; among women, intimacy sometimes results in sex." Your wife needs what we've been talking about these last few pages: kind words being spoken to her, your physical touch and presence, the feeling of connection between the two of you, to know that you value and appreciate her deeply, and that you're going to be around for the long haul. Yes, she needs these and more from you. They create in her mind and heart a kind of assurance in what the two of you have going on.

Now, sometimes the intimacy you show your wife will end in sexual relations. If that's the case, then good for you (and for her as well). However (and I think

I've mentioned this before), please don't use the intimacy you show your wife as a means to an end. You have one single motive, and that is to bless your wife. Really guard yourself from viewing your wife as an object to lust after. She is so much more valuable (to you and to God) than that. I love the words of Proverbs 5:19 which state, "She is a lovely deer, a graceful doe. Let her breasts intoxicate you all the time; always be drunk on her love" (CEB). This is a verse about faithfulness, and sexual fulfillment. Certainly I wish this for you (and your wife). But I also love the words of Proverbs 4:23 which state, "Guard your heart above all else, for it determines the course of your life" (NLT). Your wife is not an object put on this Earth to gratify your sexual desires. She is a daughter of the one true King, and was created in the image of God almighty. She is not a "thing" to be used, she is a "person" to be loved. So guard your heart, love her, and bless her.

Right now, my wife Meredith just came back from a weekend trip with her family (my in-laws). I really haven't seen her in three days. I'm sitting at our kitchen table writing this. She just put on her pajamas, got her Kindle, and headed back to our room. What this means for me is that I'd better finish up quick and go pay some attention to her, or a dead man I will be. Blessings, and see you tomorrow!

---

### *Task to Consider:*

Make out with your wife passionately and regularly.

---

# BLESS HER SENSE

*"One looks back with appreciation to the brilliant teachers, but with gratitude to those who touched our human feelings. The curriculum is so much necessary raw material, but warmth is the vital element for the growing plant and for the soul of the child"* (Carl Jung).

Marilyn Monroe once commented, "I have feelings too. I am still human. All I want is to be loved, for myself and for my talent." This week we are going to touch on this very thing – feelings. We are going to focus on the sensitivity you employ with your wife, affecting her emotional and even intellectual health. We are going to talk about your wife's woundedness, her need for safety, her need to be heard, her desire to have a life-partner with whom she can share virtually everything, what holding her can do for her well-being, and much more.

I have a strong desire to serve my country. Truth be told, I would absolutely love to be a chaplain in one of the branches of our United States armed forces. This desire became clear on September 11, 2001. In June of 2006 I was ordained as an elder in the United Methodist Church, which qualified me for service as a military chaplain, and I immediately started contacting recruiters. By July I had my entrance into the United States Army all lined out, and even had a date for an endorsement interview with my denomination in Nashville. I figured this would probably be a good time to let Meredith (who I married in 2000) know what's going on (because at that point she knew nothing). She freaked, majorly, at the idea of me joining the military. She told me, "You want to join the military as a chaplain in the US Army Reserve, and you want to start working on your doctorate. I don't want you to do both at the same time because I'll never see you. So why don't you start your doctorate, and when you finish that we can revisit the other." So I started my doctoral work in January of 2007. While I continued my studies, I had dozens of conversations with active duty and reserve soldiers, sailors, chaplains, generals, and other military personnel. When I graduated Perkins School of Theology with my Doctor of Ministry in May of 2011, I had everything lined out to continue my pursuit of a part-time career in the military. And, again, I figured this would probably be a good time to let Meredith know what's going on. And again, she freaked, majorly.

To make a very long story short, and through much conversation, listening, counseling, and prayer, I ended my pursuit of service in our military. Meredith's experience with the important men of her life is that they have a tendency to leave (either physically, or by lack of involvement in her life). And she saw me joining the military as simply another man who was walking away and leaving her and her two daughters. When I made that connection (which only took me a good five years – so much for sensitivity!), I began to understand why it had been such a sensitive subject. I got in touch with her feelings on the matter, and I knew there was only one thing I could do. I stopped the process of enlisting (again, and for good). I have a strong desire to serve my country, but I have a stronger desire to serve my wife and my family. And it took a lot for me to recognize that is exactly where God wants me to be.

God bless you, now go bless your wife!

# DAY 8 - TWO ARE BETTER THAN ONE

*"Two are better than one because they have a good return for their hard work. If either should fall, one can pick up the other. But how miserable are those who fall and don't have a companion to help them up! Also, if two lie down together, they can stay warm. But how can anyone stay warm alone? Also, one can be overpowered, but two together can put up resistance. A three-ply cord doesn't easily snap"* (Ecclesiastes 4:9-12 CEB).

*"We are all wonderful, beautiful wrecks. That's what connects us – that we're all broken, all beautifully imperfect"* (Emilio Estevez).

## Thought for the Day:

There was a thought that occasionally filled my head during my high school and college years. It was simple: "You're never going to get married." I hated that thought. I didn't want to live the single life. I wanted to find the right girl, get married, and have children with her. I knew that even when I'm lonely I'm never really alone (because of God's presence), but I didn't want to go through this life without a life-partner. I didn't want to go through this life without a wife.

The writer of Ecclesiastes knew this all too well. We need others. Men need other men who will be positive influences for us, hold us accountable, and help us grow in Christ. Proverbs 27:17 states, "As iron sharpens iron, so one person sharpens another" (NIV). However, you also need your wife, and she needs you. She needs you to pick her up when she falls. She needs you to keep her warm. She needs your loving care and support for the trials and struggles she will face in her life. She needs you to help heal her wounds, and to make her feel safe and secure. Did I mention she needs *you*?

There are so many ways to let your wife know that you are there for her and she is not alone in this world. You can intentionally spend time with her, hold her hand, take a walk or sit down, talk, and just be there with and for her. You can write her little love notes, meaningful heartfelt letters, or buy her a card to let her know just how much you value her and the marriage you share. You can communicate to her that she is beautiful, and a great treasure in your life.

The very first man on this Earth was lonely. He didn't have a life-partner. Everything God had made God called "good." But "the Lord God said, 'It is not good for the man to be alone. I will make a helper suitable for him.' Now, the Lord God had formed out of the ground all the wild animals and all the birds in the sky. He brought them to the man to see what he would name them; and whatever the man called each living creature, that was its name. So the man gave names to all the livestock, the birds in the sky and all the wild animals. But for Adam no suitable helper was found. So the Lord God caused the man to fall into a deep sleep; and while he was sleeping, he took one of the man's ribs and then closed up the place with flesh. Then the Lord God made a woman from the rib he had taken out of the man, and he brought her to the man. The man said, 'This is now bone of my bones and flesh of my flesh; she shall be called woman, for she was taken out of man.' That is why a man leaves his father and mother and is united to his wife, and they become one flesh" (Genesis 2:18-24 NIV). The Bible is clear, two are better than one!

---

### *Task to Consider:*

Write your wife a note, telling her she's beautiful and stating three reasons why you love her.

---

# DAY 9 - MAKE HER FEEL SAFE

*"Love is patient, love is kind, it isn't jealous, it doesn't brag, it isn't arrogant, Love puts up with all things, trusts in all things, hopes for all things, endures all things"* (1 Corinthians 13:4, 7 CEB).

*"If you're yelling, you're the one who's lost control of the conversation"* (Taylor Swift).

## Thought for the Day:

Just this past week I was on Cypress Lake in Bossier City, Louisiana, with my two daughters, visiting some friends. I was out in the lake, swimming around the boat dock with my girls, kayaking down the cove, and floating in a tube when a huge dark cloud blew in quickly. We got out of the water, covered the kayaks, tied up the tube, and headed for the house at the speed of, well, lightning. Dark clouds are ominous and scary. You don't mess with them, because if you do you could possibly wind up getting badly hurt. They blow up quickly, and then depart (sometimes leaving considerable collateral damage behind).

Are you a dark cloud to your wife? Are you an ominous and/or scary presence at times? Do you blow up at things your wife says or does, then leave her to feel ashamed and hurt all by herself? Are you negative, threatening, or belittling to her? Do you make her feel inferior? Do you raise your voice at her? If the answer to any of these questions is "yes," then, brother, some things need to change! Your wife wasn't given to you by God so that you could inflict more hurt and pain on her than she already has. That's not your role in her life. Your role is the total opposite.

Consider Proverbs 16:24, which states, "Pleasant words are flowing honey, sweet to the taste and healing to the bones" (CEB). I just bought a jar of honey from a local produce stand in my parents' home town of Coushatta, LA. I bought it for four reasons. One is that this particular jar of honey had the honeycomb in it (which is just cool). Secondly, it was made from a local bee whisperer (or whatever honey-making people are called). Third, my girls wanted it. Lastly, I knew just how it would taste... delicious (and it does!). When a dark cloud appears, you usually run the other way. But not so with good honey (unless you have an allergy!). You run to good honey. You generously pour it on your biscuit, in your coffee, and mix it in your oatmeal. Honey is said to have a number of healing properties as well. So let me ask you this: Do you want to be a dark cloud or honey to your wife? Rhetorical question, I know.

Paul helps us with the direction we need to go here. He tells us to love, and love is patient. Love is kind. It "bears all things, believes all things, hopes all things, and endures all things." Real love, the kind of love your wife needs from you, is a healing balm to her. She needs it. She wants it. In fact, she craves it – from you.

### *Task to Consider:*

Record the attitude you take with your wife for one week, and make some adjustments (to yourself, not her) where necessary.

# DAY 10 - LISTEN TO HER

*"Know this, my dear brothers and sisters: everyone should be quick to listen, slow to speak, and slow to grow angry"* (James 1:19 CEB).

*"Most people do not listen with the intent to understand; they listen with the intent to reply"* (Stephen R. Covey).

## Thought for the Day:

I love that quote by Stephen R. Covey. It is so true. We live in a society where listening is quickly becoming a lost art. In fact, we have to pay people to listen to us these days. When your wife is talking with you (especially if it is a tense subject), do you hear what she has to say? While she is talking, are you formulating a response in your head? When we do this, we really hear very little of what she has to say (and none of what she is saying "below the surface"). However, if we will just bite our tongue and listen, we will quickly be reminded that there are always two sides to every coin, and we will see our wife (or the person with whom you are speaking) in a new light. And strangely enough, when you listen to her, she is going to feel heard. Your wife will not care what you know until she knows that you care, and you have the perfect way to show her you care – listen!

Another thing we guys tend to do is go into "fix it" mode. Something is wrong and we just want to fix it so that it won't be wrong anymore and we can continue living in this fairytale dream where everything is OK. But your wife doesn't want you to fix it. She wants you to listen to her. She wants the emotional support that only you can give her when you listen to her worries, cares, problems, and joys.

People gripe all the time about those who talk too much, but have you ever heard someone gripe at a person who was listening too much? James tells us to be "quick to listen" and "slow to speak." This makes sense in a number of ways, but especially when you think about the biological fact that humans are born with two ears and one mouth! We should listen at least twice as much as we talk, but that is rarely the case. Calvin Coolidge once commented, "It takes a great man to be a good listener." He is right. But the good news here is that you have what it takes to be a good listener. God has put it in your heart to love your wife, to make her feel safe, and to help her feel heard. I know she talks a lot (way more than you do, in many marriages). I know her incessant ramblings wear on your nerves. I get it. I'm use to it too! But patience, my friend. What she has to say is important. And your wife having a life-partner who is willing to listen to her is equally important.

---

### *Task to Consider:*

Listen to your wife in such a way that you can repeat back everything to her that she just said (this is called *mirroring*).

---

# DAY 11 - TALK "FEELINGS" WITH HER

*"Be happy with those who are happy, and cry with those
who are crying"* (Romans 12:15 CEB).

*"Loneliness is the first thing which God's eye named not good"* (John Milton).

## Thought for the Day:

"Oh no, not that. Anything but that. We can talk about my promotion, my boat, fishing, football, basketball, baseball, the car, the kids, and even create a Home Depot shopping list together. But I just can't talk feelings with her!!!" My friend, I'm here to say you can, and you must.

Paul is clear that we must be empathetic towards one another. Jesus knew this well also (check out John 11:35). I would say this is critical for those who are married. When your wife is sad, she needs to get that out. When your wife is overjoyed, she needs to get that out. Are you there for her? Can you walk that line with and for her? Does she know that she can come home with good news, bad news, the bullet points of a crummy day, or the intel that her mom's trip to your house will last one week longer than she had originally stated?

There is this affective side to women that many many men just do not get. We are macho. We are tough. We don't cry. We don't get too happy. Maybe we got a little crazy back when we were adolescents, but now we just mutter things under our breath, grunt, scratch, and go to work. Sorry, man, but that's just not going to cut it. Your wife needs you to:

- Be sensitive toward her.
- Know how critical communication is to her.

- Spend time with her (the more, the merrier!).
- Appreciate her for who she is.
- Show her that you are on her team.
- Affirm her.
- Seek to understand where she's coming from.

And when you do these things you will build her trust in you, fulfill her desire for closeness, dissolve her fears, and make her feel loved and respected. All of this is very hard (and we will probably never truly get why it is so important), but she can feel so lonely and she needs you to be there for her.

Job is a figure in the Old Testament who suffered terribly. He lost his wealth. All of his children were killed. And he was inflicted with painful sores all over his body. Job 2:11 states, "When Job's three friends heard about all this disaster that had happened to him, they came, each one from his home—Eliphaz from Teman, Bildad from Shuah, and Zophar from Naamah. They agreed to come so they could console and comfort him" (CEB). For seven days they just sat with Job, saying nothing. Your wife needs no less from you.

---

### *Task to Consider:*

Ask your wife, "How are you feeling:  mad, sad, glad, scared?"

---

# DAY 12 - HOLD HER

*"His left arm is beneath my head, his right embraces me"*
(Song of Songs 2:6 CEB).

*"When I come home, my daughter will run to the door and give me a big hug, and everything that's happened that day just melts away"* (Hugh Jackman).

## Thought for the Day:

One of the great ways that you can give your wife emotional support is to hold her. The embrace is such a powerful form of communication. In it a couple experiences warmth, love, joy, trust, and safety. It is a physical reminder that we are not alone in this world, that we have someone to lean on, we are not isolated, and that we have someone who will walk through this life with us.

Holding is easy – and it is free! There is no complicated formula that accompanies it. You don't have to figure anything or anyone out. You don't even have to talk. You just hold, squeeze (not too tight!), and connect. That's what a good hug actually does for a married couple. Whatever is going on, and wherever you have been, when a man and a woman come together, a long hug serves as the perfect way to reconnect with one another. It is a silent form of saying, "I love you, and I'm here for you." It is intimate, blissful, and necessary. You can get lost in it, caught up in it, and it makes time stand still. Holding relaxes a person, strengthens the immune system, reduces stress, releases tension, helps us to breathe, boosts self-esteem, elevates our mood, and is terrific therapy (and has zero negative side effects!). Hugging also just feels good (more like amazing!).

I love the children's poem by Shel Silverstein entitled, "Hug O' War":

*I will not play at tug o' war.*
*I'd rather play at hug o' war,*
*Where everyone hugs*
*Instead of tugs,*
*Where everyone giggles*
*And rolls on the rug,*
*Where everyone kisses,*
*And everyone grins,*
*And everyone cuddles,*
*And everyone wins.*

This poem simply captures what your wife desires. It captures the essence of an embrace. Because you both truly win when you hug. You have the opportunity to give and receive. That passionate embrace is glue for your marriage, and the sign of a healthy home. So I encourage you, "Hug early and often!"

---

### *Task to Consider:*
Give your wife a <u>minimum</u> of four hugs per day
(and start working towards ten per day).

---

# DAY 13 - CAPTURE YOUR THOUGHTS

*"... capture every thought to make it obedient to Christ"* (2 Corinthians 10:5 CEB).

*"Once you replace negative thoughts with positive ones,*
*you'll start having positive results"* (Willie Nelson).

## Thought for the Day:

I've heard it said that the human mind processes 40 to 80 thousand thoughts each and every day. That's a lot of thinking. I can hardly begin to think about thinking that much, and maybe that statistic is for people with brains more evolved than mine! But if this is true, what is it that we think about 40 to 80 thousand times a day? What fills our head? Worry? Anxiety? Jealousy? Anger? Addictive tendencies? Negativity? Possibly with a few pleasant thoughts?

You've heard the saying, "Garbage in, garbage out." It's true. What we consume with our senses forms us and changes us. And this affects not just us, but those around us as well. Meredith just got back from a spiritual pilgrimage to Iona, Scotland. One comment that she has made to me since her return is how she has no desire to watch the news. Now, this is remarkable, because Meredith would watch the news every night before going to bed. But now, tuning in to all the horrible things happening in our world that we can do nothing about (which in turn causes incredible anxiety, among other effects) is something she is just not that interested in. She is interested in doing what she can with those around her. She is interested in shining light in the dark corners here where we live. She is interested in blessing those who cross her path. She is more peaceful, and more alive. Amazing! Garbage in, garbage out.

And we guys consume media that is so much more harmful than the evening news, don't we? You watch a horror movie, and you have to look behind the shower curtain before you go to the bathroom. Not that I know this from personal experience... So maybe what we need to do is to fill our minds with thoughts that are good, wholesome, pure, and holy. Now, this is hard for me, because I love good science fiction, action, thriller, killin' movies. Manly movies. But what I've also learned is that these films have a tendency of leaving disturbing images in my head that take years to get out (if at all). I also worry a lot (and that's putting it lightly). So something I've practiced most of my conscious life (and even more since I discovered Dr. Gary Smalley's book entitled *Guarding Your Child's Heart*[3]) is capturing my thoughts.

When I get angry or start thinking negative thoughts (about something that is totally out of my control), here are a few things I do to capture them and find peace (**Task to Consider**):

- Repeat a Short Prayer - For example, if I'm in a conflict with someone, I normally repeat the words "God, make this right."
- Recite a Scripture - This is one great reason to spend time memorizing passages from the Bible, so you can have truth ready to dispel the bad thoughts that come.
- Reach Out to a Friend - I am a verbal processor, and I've found it very helpful to talk through my baggage with a trusted friend who knows how to listen.
- Record Your Thoughts - When I find myself overwhelmed with bad thoughts, I go to my journal and write it out. I only do this a few times a year, but, man, does it help.

---

3 Smalley, Gary. *Guarding Your Child's Heart: Establish Your Child's Faith Through Scripture Memory and Meditation* (Colorado Springs: NavPress, 2011).

# DAY 14 - FINISH THE RACE WITH HER

*"I have fought the good fight, finished the race, and kept the faith"*
(2 Timothy 4:7 CEB).

*"It is really rare to find someone you really, really love and that you want to
spend your life with and all that stuff that goes along with being married.
I am one of those lucky people. And I think she feels that way too.
So the romantic stuff is easy because you want them to be happy"*
(Harry Connick, Jr.).

## Thought for the Day:

A good friend of mine regularly says this or that is not "blessed with eternal life."
Although I love that statement (and use it often myself), it doesn't apply to the
marriage covenant. Of course I'm not sure what happens in Heaven with people
who are married on Earth (Jesus has something to say about this in Mark 12:18
to 27!), but the point I'm making here is that you should never even begin to consider putting an end to your marriage. When Paul is writing to Timothy, he uses
illustrations like a race and a great battle to exemplify how he kept the Christian
faith even in dark times. In your marriage you too must fight the good fight, finish the race, and remain faithful to your wife always. If the greatest behaviors we
can display in our life here on Earth are to "love God and love our neighbors as
ourself," then staying faithful to God has something to do with staying faithful
to our closest neighbor – our wife.

If you are thinking about divorcing your wife, I encourage you to rethink that.
Do you realize that your marriage has the potential to change the world? Do you
know that she needs you desperately (and if she is the one initiating the divorce
proceedings, then I encourage you to fight for her with all your might – don't go

into that night quietly). Don't break that promise you made to her, to God, and to every man and woman who attended your wedding. Stick with her through thick and thin. Go to hell and back for her. Finish that race!

Now, I realize that there might be some good reasons to end a marriage. I've been working with couples for close to 15 years now, and I've seen many marriages end in divorce. These have been parishioners, acquaintances, family members, and some close friends. It makes me sick and I hate to see this happen. I'm a child of divorced parents. Meredith is a child of divorced parents. It's ugly and hurtful to the couple, as well as the rest of the family (and certainly to any children involved). I've come to know three "A's" that can end a marriage promptly: Affairs, Abuse, and Addictions. So I say to you, whoever you are, stay away from these three. If you are engaged in any of them, end it now. Get away from that other woman, go to counseling, AA, or some other accountability group; but end it. Because of these, and other situations, I know that some marriages will end in divorce. Because of these, and other situations, some marriages need to end in divorce. That being said, the power of God is stronger than any challenge you will ever face in your marriage. The Holy Spirit can bring reconciliation to any relationship that has experienced damage. I tell couples often, "God's power is stronger than what you are going through right now. You can't stay the same. You must make some changes here. But God will give you the power to do it. God wants your marriage to remain intact even more than you want it to." I believe this with all my heart. So fight the good fight, finish the race, and keep the faith; not just with Jesus, but with your wife.

---

### Task to Consider:

Stick with your wife for life, and regularly tell her that she's stuck with you.

---

# BLESS HER STATUS

*"My dad taught me from my youngest childhood memories through these connections*
*with Aboriginal and tribal people that you must always*
*protect people's sacred status, regardless of the past"*
(Bindi Irwin, daughter of Steve "The Crocodile Hunter" Irwin).

This week we are going to be talking about your wife's status, her social health, her place in the world. We'll be taking up such topics as communication (and creating a vision for your marriage), cherishing your wife (think about those traditional vows), being her biggest fan, validating her work, dating her, and even giving her some space. We'll come across more challenges to being a "status quo" husband (which just isn't cutting it), but I know you're game.

One of the primary thoughts I have when I think about blessing our wives in an unconditional "with no strings attached" kind of way deals completely with a powerful perspective we take towards our lives. As husbands we want to honor God first, and also honor our wives (loving them as we love ourselves). To do this, however, we need to follow the advice of Proverbs 4:23 which states, "Guard your heart above all else, for it determines the course of your life" (Proverbs 4:23 NLT). Three little words I encourage you to memorize are "guard your heart." *Guard your heart.* It is the wellspring of life. So from what might we as husbands need to guard our hearts? What is laying siege to our hearts? I think a one-word answer is "temptation." We are tempted on all sides. We are tempted to put ourselves first always, and to think that the universe revolves around us. We are tempted to think that our wives are second in line to our superior gender. However, I'm pretty sure that Jesus would call this sin. And if we're not making ourselves god of the universe, we make idols of status, power, position, prestige, money, and material possessions. What else? As if that's not enough! We are tempted to give our heart to other women through extramarital affairs (which usually begin as innocent interactions with the opposite sex, but move beyond that quickly), and also through addiction to pornography, alcohol, drugs, gambling, or even sports.

We all struggle with sin, and we are all broken men. So don't fool yourself. It comforts me to read the Apostle Paul talk about his struggles as he writes, "And I know that nothing good lives in me, that is, in my sinful nature. I want to do what is right, but I can't. I want to do what is good, but I don't. I don't want to do what is wrong, but I do it anyway. I have discovered this principle of life—that when I want to do what is right, I inevitably do what is wrong. Oh, what a miserable person I am! Who will free me from this life that is dominated by sin and death? Thank God! The answer is in Jesus Christ our Lord" (Romans 7:18, 19, 21, 24, 25 NLT). So what are we to do with all of these temptations? My friend, you need to dig into God's Word (the Bible) and immerse your mind in the mind of God. You need to pray to our Father in Heaven, and immerse your heart in the heart of God. And you need to run. Run, Forest, run. That's what you need to do. You need to run to God and from whatever is tempting you. James states, "Therefore, submit to God. Resist the devil, and he will run away from you." (James 4:7 CEB).

If you are interested in blessing your wife with no strings attached, you must work on dealing with your own personal sin. The truth is, there is only One who can help you with that (and it ain't me!). Confess your temptations and sin to Jesus, because "... if we confess our sins, he is faithful and just to forgive us our sins and cleanse us from everything we've done wrong" (1 John 1:9 CEB).

God bless you, now go bless your wife!

# DAY 15 - COMMUNICATE WITH HER

*"When there's no vision, the people get out of control"* (Proverbs 29:18 CEB).

*"It really boils down to this: that all life is interrelated. We are all caught in an inescapable network of mutuality, tied into a single garment of destiny. Whatever affects one destiny, affects all indirectly"* (Dr. Martin Luther King, Jr.).

## Thought for the Day and Task to Consider:

Where is your marriage going? I'm sure at this point in the life you are making with your wife and family you have had some great times and some rocky times. There have been moments of laughter and excitement, along with moments of pain and misery. But where is your marriage going from this point forward? Are you going to let it just be blown here and there by the wind? Are you going to take the attitude of "whatever will be will be?" Or are you going to be intentional and, together with your wife, give your marriage some direction? Now, I know the Bible tells us that we can make all kinds of plans, but in the end God directs our steps (Proverbs 16:9), and another proverb states, "Man plans, God laughs." However, we simply cannot use this as an excuse to not give some "vision" to our marriage.

So I have a couple of thoughts that go along with this necessary work. The first is to take Dr. King's advice and acknowledge that you and your wife are intricately connected. The relationship you have with her has the potential of changing the lives of those around you for the better. The ripples your marriage makes in the world for good can truly have no end. Not only that, but if you invest in blessing your wife, your marriage will have a better chance of creating a healthy home, which will develop healthy children, who will go forth from that home to bless the world.[4] But it all comes down to the two of you, husband and wife, being in this together (and regularly engaging in healthy communication). The relationship that you have is mutual, reciprocal, and interdependent. I encourage you to get over all of this "equality" kind of thinking that promotes, "I'll give 50% if she gives 50%." That's baloney, and will never work! You work on giving 100%, bless her daily with no strings attached, and just trust that she will do the same. And don't criticize her when she doesn't come through, because I promise you won't always come through either. But love her, communicate with her, dream with her, and create this plan with her because YOU NEED HER (and she needs you, and the world needs your marriage).

So after getting that straight, the next thought is to be SMART about your Marriage Vision. Set some goals that are:

**Specific** - Make them clear (and answer who, what, when, where, why, and how).

**Measurable** - Include criteria that will allow you to assess your progress.

**Attainable** - Keep them realistic, not too challenging (and not too easy).

**Relevant** - Stay on topic.

**Time Bound** - Pick a deadline, and celebrate your progress!

Here's a sample – "My wife and I will go on a date by ourselves once a week because we know this time of connection is vital to the health of our marriage. Each Sunday evening we will plan our date, and then schedule a babysitter to watch the children." Now it's your turn!

---

4  My friend, mentor, and fellow Sci-Fi buff Dr. Harville Hendrix introduced me to this concept.

# DAY 16 - CHERISH HER

*"As for husbands, love your wives just like Christ loved
the church and gave himself for her"* (Ephesians 5:25 CEB).

*"Let the wife make the husband glad to come home, and let
him make her sorry to see him leave"* (Martin Luther).

## Thought for the Day:

If there is anything you truly want for your wife, at the top of that list is for her
to feel cherished. To feel like she is enough, adequate, and sufficient. To feel safe.
To feel treasured. To feel loved. It's been said that "love is a verb." Love is also
hard, because to do it right takes consistency (which is hard for undisciplined
folks like me!). Whether or not you are feeling love towards (or from) your wife
on any given day, are you able to make her feel cherished? Are you able to show
your fondness and affection towards her? That is a good personal goal for you to
have in your marriage. And it will make all the difference to her.

Let's take a look at those traditional vows that grooms recite at weddings:
*"In the name of God, I _____, take you, _____, to be my wife,*
*to have and to hold from this day forward,*
*for better, for worse, for richer, for poorer,*
*in sickness and in health, to love and to cherish,*
*until we are parted by death.*
*This is my solemn vow."*[5]

---

5  *The United Methodist Book of Worship* (Nashville: The United Methodist Publishing House,
1992), pg. 120.

Perhaps you said something like this to your wife on your wedding day. And perhaps you understood what you were saying then, and perhaps you didn't. So today, let me remind you of a promise you made (not a contract you signed). It's a promise you celebrate each year on your anniversary. It's a promise you made to your wife, to God, and to every person who attended your wedding. It is a promise you want to keep. And part of that promise is "to love and to cherish" your wife. Are you being faithful to that promise? Are you loving her the way that Jesus Christ "loved the church and gave himself for her"?

One of the ways that I have found to cherish my wife is through spontaneous gift-giving. Meredith's primary love language is receiving gifts, so when I bless her with some token of my affection (whether big or small, it really doesn't matter), she feels loved. This morning as I was literally heading out the door to the office, I took a little piece of paper and wrote on it, "You are lovely and beautiful." I drew a small heart, wrote my initials on it, and then placed it on the dashboard of her car. This might have taken me about 10 seconds to do, but I know that it'll make her feel cherished for the whole day (unless I mess it up by saying something critical or negative to her later!). Now, I told you before, I'm not an expert at this stuff. But this isn't rocket science either. Just love your wife. Make her feel adored. Care for her. Nurture her. Cherish her. You've got what it takes.

---

### Task to Consider:

Write your wife a short love note.

---

# DAY 17 - ENCOURAGE HER

*"I can do all things through Christ who strengthens me"* (Philippians 4:13 NKJV).

*"Our chief want is someone who will inspire us to be what we know we could be"* (Ralph Waldo Emerson).

## Thought for the Day:

Two, four, six, eight, who do you appreciate? I hope you appreciate your wife! God knows she needs it. It's so interesting, as I was doing some research for this day's devotion I came across article after article on how we don't need to worry about the opinions of others. And as much as I agree with that thought, we all need to know that somebody is there in our corner rooting for us, cheering us on. We all need a biggest fan. Are you your wife's biggest fan? My friend, she already has enough critics (and she is her worst enemy). What she needs from you is encouragement. She needs to know that she has what it takes, that she is an amazing and beautiful woman, that she is a good wife, that she is a loving mother, that she is a hard worker. If you don't give her this encouragement, where else will she get it? And you certainly don't want her getting it only from other men!

You have a major calling and an incredible opportunity before you. You get to be the physical representation of Jesus Christ to your wife. In fact, you can actually be Christ to your wife when you bless her in this way (which is pretty cool). You get to remind her that she can do all things through Christ who gives her strength (Philippians 4:13). You get to remind her that nothing is impossible for God (Luke 1:37). You get to believe in her with all your might. You get to help her relax in the assurance that she is a child of God almighty, and nothing can separate her from God's love in Jesus Christ our Lord (Romans 8:38). You get to be the one who informs her (at times when she is feeling insecure and stressed) that she will never be able to please everyone, that focusing on "what is" will always be preferable to focusing on "what might be," and that she is creating imagined scenarios in her mind that are wasting her time, energy, and imagination. You get to hold her accountable to the boundaries that she has set. You get to assist her in staying grounded (which includes hitting the "pause" button at times). And best of all, you get to encourage her to be her, because there is only one of her in the entire world. Talk about a high calling! Are you up for this?

Your wife is a powerhouse. She is so strong, confident, and secure. However, life has a tendency of chipping away at each and every one of us. After a while the strain (or the pain) becomes too much and we get low, we cave, we become depressed. Dr. Seuss commented, "Be who you are and say what you feel because those who mind don't matter and those who matter don't mind." I hope you are one of the people in your wife's life who are in the "matter" category. Love her, support her, and encourage her. When she's up, when she's down, and even when you are unsure, uncertain, and maybe even a little scared as to the particular mood she's in; just be there for her. As Paul writes, "So continue encouraging each other and building each other up, just like you are doing already" (1 Thessalonians 5:11 CEB).

---

### Task to Consider:

Ask your wife about her dreams, and how you can help her fulfill them (then constantly encourage and assure her that she's got what it takes).

---

# DAY 18 - VALIDATE HER

*"Whatever you do, do it from the heart for the
Lord and not for people"* (Colossians 3:23 CEB).

*"The deepest principle of human nature is the craving to be appreciated"*
(William James).

## Thought for the Day:

Another way to bless your wife is to validate her. Not only does she need to be told that she is valuable, but also that what she is doing, feeling, and experiencing is valid. Men yearn to be respected, and one of the primary ways we receive that is through verbal validations. The truth is, your wife needs to hear those kinds of words too. She struggles, just like you, to balance all the many facets of her life. And at the end of the day (or even the beginning of it!), she would be thrilled to hear that what she is going through is worthwhile and has great merit. And guess what? That's where you come in!

So there are three primary areas that I'd like to talk about validating your wife today. The first is her work. Whether she works primarily in the home (which means she is probably driving all over the country for you and your children) or outside of the home, remind her that what she is doing is so valuable. The effort she puts in makes such a difference in your life, in the lives of your children, and those in her business. Your lives would be so very different if it were not for her work. Maybe she is working outside the home because you two are young professionals, because you can't survive financially on one income, or because she just likes to have a career. Whatever the case is, it really doesn't matter. Let her know that she's a rock star and that her work matters. If her work is primarily in the home and with the family, then let her know that she's a rock star and that her work matters.

Another way to appreciate her is to validate her feelings. When she talks to you, listen to her. She has something important to say (even if it's not important to you), and deeply desires to be heard. Again, you'd rather her be having these conversations with you than with some other guy! So stop what you're doing, drop the remote or latest hunting magazine you're reading (or probably just looking at), and roll with it. I know you have empathy in you. Compassion is your bag. So put it to use and let her know that you are there for her to hear whatever in the world she has to say (even if it totally makes no sense to you and goes completely over your head). Stick with her. Let her know that you're tracking, that she's not crazy, and that what she's saying makes very good sense.

A third way to appreciate her is to validate her sense of being overwhelmed. The constant struggle to keep all the balls in the air takes a toll on your wife. There will be moments when she breaks, and she needs you desperately. Just be there, let her tears soak through your favorite shirt, hold her, hold her some more, let her cry as long as she needs to, and don't try to fix anything. Remember Job's three friends who came to comfort him during a time of intense pain (Job 2)? He experienced some healing as they sat with him in silence for seven straight days. But then they began trying to fix Job, and it made his situation so much worse. We can learn a lesson from that. So get to work, and honor God through the way you validate your wife.

---

### Task to Consider:
Stop trying to control your wife, and start validating her.

---

# DAY 19 - DATE HER

*"Rejoice in the wife of your youth"* (Proverbs 5:18 CEB).

*"Love seems the swiftest but it is the slowest of all growths. No man or woman really knows what perfect love is until they have been married a quarter of a century"* (Mark Twain).

## Thought for the Day and Several Tasks to Consider:

OK, so if I was to get a grade on "dating" my wife, I would get an F. Courtship after marriage is something with which I struggle. Perhaps it's one way that evidences me taking Meredith for granted. Perhaps it's because we work a lot on the weekends. Great excuse, Bell! Perhaps I'm too focused on the things we are going to do as a family (I mean the four of us: Meredith, myself, and our two daughters). And perhaps I just need to do a better job, secure a babysitter, and plan a date. One thing is for sure, dating (your wife!) proves the statement, "love isn't something you feel, it's something you do." The truth is, the more you do love, the more you will feel it. And there are not many better ways to do love in your marriage than to court your wife. When Meredith and I go on a date together, it makes all the difference. Her eyes light up. Our conversation is deeper. We are actually able to finish a sentence without being interrupted by our children. And our intimacy grows. I guess that's why smart men plan a weekly date with their wife. And maybe I just need to learn something from them!

So here are a few thoughts I have about you dating your wife:

- Institute a regular date night - Maybe the two of you take turns planning it, but you pioneer the way. Get it kicked off, and plan the first one. Make all the arrangements. Now, your date doesn't have to be fancy or expensive. The main goal is quality time together. You can get coffee, have a picnic, or go biking. One of the last dates Meredith and I went on ended up with the two of us kayaking on Lake Grapevine. It was free, and it was a blast. You can also make a reservation, get dressed up, wash and gas up your truck, and go somewhere nice. Dating is also a perfect way to make memories together.

- Buy your wife flowers - Right now I know a dozen stores where I can buy a dozen roses for a dozen bucks, and I frequent those places. And pull a little switch-a-roo on your wife. Buy her some red roses one day, white another day, yellow, then maybe tulips instead. Mix it up.
- Watch your language - Tell your wife, "I love you," and give her daily compliments.
- Open the door for her - This is a super easy way to let her know she matters.
- Take her on a weekend getaway - Just the two of you.
- Spend twenty minutes on the couch talking, connecting, and being with each other.
- Make her coffee in the morning - Pour her a cup, doctor it up, and take it to her.
- Never underestimate the power of spontaneity - Surprise her with a lunch date, a note, a card, or some other token of your love.
- Ask your wife to create a "wish list" for you of things she would like to receive.
- Create together a "dream list" of activities you would like to accomplish together.
- Attend a Bible study together - Whether it focuses on a book of the Bible, marriage, parenting, or some other topic; it'll be like a date and you'll both grow in your faith.
- Hold your wife's hand.
- When you are with her, be with her - Put away your phone, laptop, etc.
- Freshen up your physical intimacy - Try something new. Get a little crazy. And use your bed for more than sleeping.

# DAY 20 - GIVE HER SOME SPACE

*"As iron sharpens iron, so a friend sharpens a friend"* (Proverbs 27:17 NLT).

*"I'm not as angry as I used to be. But I can get in touch with that anger pretty quickly if I feel my space is being invaded or somebody is not treating me with the respect that I want"* (Samuel L. Jackson).

## Thought for the Day:

This thought is pretty simple. Your wife's world is bigger than you and your children. The totality of her life cannot and should not be wrapped up in you. She needs time to herself and time with her friends. This is good. This is healthy. Codependency is very unhealthy for a couple, and is noticeable when the two of you seem to be fused together and unable to spend any spare time apart. Or perhaps you don't want her to spend any of her spare time alone or with friends because you think she should spend that time with you. If that's the case, then you are being jealous and controlling (which is a far cry from blessing). Two words: "Stop it!"

I'm not saying that you need to cut your wife off. And I'm certainly not talking here about marital separation or encouraging your wife to move out. I'm just saying that her life is bigger than you (as important as you are). One great way to love and bless your wife is to free her up to spend some time alone or with her friends. If you have children, then watch them. If not, then you can go spend some time alone or with your friends too (and I know you like to do that!). And there are some clear warning signs that let you know it just might be time for you to love your wife in this way, including: irritability, stress, fatigue, and general unhappiness.

Your wife needs time alone. This time allows her to have some space to reconnect with God, get her mind straight, get focused and centered, have some fun, get some exercise, and relax. Your wife also needs time with her girlfriends. These women are so important to her. She needs the time with them to talk, to laugh, to bond, to just be herself. And they need time with her.

Meredith loves time with her girlfriends, her sisters, and her mom. They really do sharpen each other when they are together. Meredith also loves time alone. She loves to read, and she loves to watch shows on television (she's watching the "Robin Hood" series on Netflix right now). And I'll admit it, this is frustrating to me at times. It irritates me because I'd kind of like her to give that time to me. But I've also come to the place that I understand why she needs this space and downtime. It isn't as much of a luxury as it is a necessity. It's good for her. It's good for me too.

---

### *Task to Consider:*

Free your wife up to spend some time alone or with her friends.

---

# DAY 21 - SURROUND HER WITH POSITIVE INFLUENCES

*"Plans fail for lack of counsel, but with many advisers they succeed"*
(Proverbs 15:22 NIV).

*"The key is to keep company only with people who uplift you,*
*whose presence calls forth your best"* (Epictetus).

## Thought for the Day:

I love this comment from Epictetus above, and I also love what George Washington has to say about the topic of keeping company. He states, "Associate with men of good quality if you esteem your own reputation; for it is better to be alone than in bad company." My friend, you need to surround yourself with many advisers who will offer you wise counsel (whether you want it or not!), because we are known by the company we keep. There was a time in my life when I realized that if I kept hanging around the crowd I was hanging around, then I was going to continue acting more and more like them. The problem was, I didn't want to act like them. I didn't want to be a part of a drug culture, because I had a vision for my future (and drugs would severely hinder that vision). I didn't want to aimlessly and ambivalently wander through this life. I wanted to do great things, make my life count, and help people. I didn't want to believe that this life was all about me and mine, because my faith told me something very different. So I got away from that crowd (and believe me, that's <u>not</u> when I went to seminary!). I started spending time with guys who wanted to make something of their lives, lived purposefully, dared to dream, and trusted God for the outcome. Some of these guys I found in my college social fraternity, Tau Kappa Epsilon. Some of them I became acquainted with in a Bible study. Others I befriended in swimming class at Louisiana State University in Shreveport. One was the assistant registrar at my school. Another was my resident director and boss in the men's dorm at Centenary College of Louisiana (where I first started doing "men's ministry") And, yes, some were in my family. These men became some of my best teachers, mentors, and friends. I needed them. Their place in my life was so important (and still is). Having men like this is so important for you. Having men like this in your life is so important for your wife as well. Like it's been said, "Who keeps company with wolves will learn to howl." I'm just thinking that kind of behavior isn't very impressive (or helpful) to your wife!

Time and time again the Bible urges us to be careful of the company we keep:

- "The truly happy person doesn't follow wicked advice, doesn't stand on the road of sinners, and doesn't sit with the disrespectful" (Psalms 1:1 CEB).
- "Walk with wise people and become wise; befriend fools and get in trouble" (Proverbs 13:20 CEB).
- "Don't be deceived, bad company corrupts good character" (1 Corinthians 15:33 CEB).
- "Let's also think about how to motivate each other to show love and to do good works. Don't stop meeting together with other believers, which some people have gotten into the habit of doing. Instead, encourage each other, especially as you see the day drawing near" (Hebrews 10:24, 25 CEB).

One way to surround your wife with positive influences is to surround yourself with them. Now, I'm not telling you to control who she spends time with, I'm telling you to control the people with whom YOU spend time.

---

### Task to Consider:

Make a list of the people with whom you spend time.
Do they call forth your best?

# BLESS HER SOUL

*"The Creator arranged things so that we need each other"* (Basil of Caesarea).

For the next few pages, I'd like to focus on how you can bless your wife spiritually. She is a beautiful spiritual creature with an eternal soul. Just like every other human being, and as Saint Augustine of Hippo (you just gotta love a guy with a zoo animal name!) put it so eloquently, her heart is restless until it finds rest in God. She has an innate, natural, and consistent desire to connect with God. Her soul rejoices to be in communion with her Creator, Savior, and Sustainer. The intimacy that exists between Father, Son, and Holy Spirit attracts her, and she longs to participate in that holy relationship. So we are going to talk about praying with your wife, forgiving her, worshipping with her, engaging in spiritual conversations with her, helping her to get enough rest, trusting her, and loving her as Christ loves the Church.

One topic I'm going to bring up in this introduction is something that has been highly debated in the 21st century and often abused by men throughout the course of history. It stems from Genesis 3:16, which states, "To the woman he said, 'I will make your pregnancy very painful; in pain you will bear children. You will desire your husband, but he will rule over you'" (CEB). Ephesians 5:22 and 23 state, "For example, wives should submit to their husbands as if to the Lord. A husband is the head of his wife like Christ is head of the church, that is, the savior of the body"

(CEB). Some men in the Church have decided that these verses (and others like them) should lead us to believe that men are superior to women, husbands must dominate their wives, and men are the only spiritual leaders of the home. My friend, such belief is simply not supported by scripture. The Bible doesn't give us permission to bully our wives; it encourages us to bless them. We are men, not patriarchs! In fact, neither the husband nor the wife is called in scripture to be the "spiritual leader" of the home – that's the Holy Spirit's job! Paul writes, "I say be guided by the Spirit and you won't carry out your selfish desires" (Galatians 5:16 CEB). If we want to bear fruit for the Kingdom of God, then we must be in step with the Spirit (not in the driver's seat!). Furthermore, Paul emphatically comments, "There is neither Jew nor Greek; there is neither slave nor free; nor is there male and female, for you are all one in Christ Jesus" (Galatians 3:28 CEB). And what did Jesus have to say about power? Jesus states, "You know that those who rule the Gentiles show off their authority over them and their high-ranking officials order them around. But that's not the way it will be with you. Whoever wants to be great among you will be your servant. Whoever wants to be first among you will be your slave" (Matthew 20:25-27 CEB). Perhaps we need to stop all this mess about who needs or gets to be first, and start focusing on serving.

Husbands and wives live in an interdependent relationship. Both have great responsibilities in the home and family. Both are equally called to serve. Both are equally called to love. Your responsibility to your wife is to love her so much that your marriage encourages her to love God with everything she has. Your responsibility is to be a spiritual friend to her, not just a lover, provider, and/or business partner. Your responsibility is to work with your wife in forming your children spiritually. Your responsibility is to keep yourself emotionally and spiritually grounded so you can be a rock for your family. But most important, your responsibility is to be guided by the Holy Spirit of God so that you won't live according to your own personal selfish desires. This is the true leadership that your family desperately needs, with no strings attached.

God bless you, now go bless your wife!

# DAY 22 - PRAY WITH HER

*"For this reason, confess your sins to each other and pray for each other
so that you may be healed. The prayer of the righteous person is powerful
in what it can achieve"* (James 5:16 CEB).

*"God shapes the world by prayer. The more praying there is in the world,
the better the world will be"* (E. M. Bounds).

## Thought for the Day:

If you'd like to increase the intimacy in your marriage, then pray for your wife.
Pray for her in your daily prayers (whenever you spend time in prayer: morning,
night, throughout the day). Ask God to continue blessing her and making her
more and more like Christ. Ask God to give you all you need to be the husband
she needs, and to open your eyes and heart to new ways to be even more of a
blessing to her. Pray for her workload, her life as a mother, what stresses her out,
and your marriage. Lift it all up to God in prayer.

Now take this a step farther. Pray with your wife. I have learned how powerful prayer can be when you stop what you are doing and pray for someone in
need. In a world that is defined by words like "blur" and "noise," two people
praying together is one of the only things I've found that can actually stop the
clock. Nothing else matters. For a few moments you are focused on God's presence, that other person, and what God is doing through you to minister to that
other person. I find myself (when my head is on straight) being mindful that
some person with whom I'm speaking just might appreciate someone praying
for them (and what's funny is that these people usually give us all the clues we
need to know that they need prayer). And instead of throwing out that overused
Christian phrase "I'll pray for you." (which is a lie because we don't do it), why

not just ask them right then and there if you can pray for them? My experience is that the great majority of the time people will not turn you down. I've found myself praying with other people in my office, in hallways, in stores, on sidewalks. I know those prayers are meaningful to those people. But those times have also on many occasions been the highlight of my day.

So like I said, let's take this a step farther. Let's not just talk about "those people out there." Let's talk about your wife. In your conversations with her (hopefully you are making time to have some of these!), listen to what she is saying. Is she overwhelmed, frustrated, or afraid? Is she elated, overjoyed, amazed? Is she trying to make a big decision, and struggling on what she needs to do? One way to let her know that you care, that you are listening, and that you are there for her is to pray with her. Stop everything. Ask her if you can pray with her (she might be shocked, but she'll get over it!), hold her hands, and pray. If you are on the phone, then you can do the same thing (minus the holding hands part). You can even send her texts throughout the day letting her know that you are continuing to pray for her.

You can set aside a time each day to do this with your wife, and/or you can look for those opportunities to lift her up to God in prayer. Either way, it will bless her soul.

---

### Task to Consider:

Ask your wife how you can pray for her, hold her hands, and pray together.

---

# DAY 23 - FORGIVE HER

*"Be tolerant with each other and, if someone has a complaint against anyone, forgive each other. As the Lord forgave you, so also forgive each other"*
(Colossians 3:13 CEB).

*"A happy marriage is the union of two good forgivers"* (Robert Quillen).

## Thought for the Day:

We all (men and women) are broken people. We all have scars and wounds. We all mess up (and it's not like this is just a thing of the past, because it keeps happening!). We all at times react instead of responding, and sometimes our behavior and words cause great harm. Like Paul reminds us, "All have sinned and fall short of God's glory" (Romans 3:23 CEB). We are all in the same boat. But the good news of our faith is that "God demonstrates His own love toward us, in that while we were yet sinners, Christ died for us" (Romans 5:8 NASB). We have been forgiven by God, and perhaps that's an example we can follow with our wives.

There are things your wife has done (or not done) that cause you to be bitter and resentful towards her. Maybe it was something totally innocent on her part, but it hurt you nonetheless. Maybe she knew exactly what she was doing. Maybe she just got carried away as the tension rose. Maybe she has apologized, and maybe she hasn't. Maybe it was a bad decision she made. Maybe she did something that made you feel disrespected. Regardless of the specifics of the situation, you harbor some ill feelings toward your wife because of this. It's possible that you even have trouble trusting her.

What would it look like to offer your wife forgiveness for the pain she has caused you? To give her the benefit of the doubt and trust that she truly loves you? To realize that she is a flawed human being (just like you), but she is doing her very best. I love the statement Lewis B. Smedes has made on forgiveness, "To forgive is to set a prisoner free and discover that the prisoner was you." Maybe you need to meet with your pastor, a spiritual director, and/or a professional counselor. Maybe you just need to spend some time with a trusted friend who can help you work though your feelings. Maybe you need to spend some time with God, giving him your hurts, pain, and anger. However you choose to address this, release and freedom come to the man who chooses to forgive his wife. Joy comes to the man who chooses to lovingly embrace his wife for who she is, warts and all (not that your wife has warts!).

And what if your wife refuses to stop the behavior that is hurtful to you? You can't make your wife change. That is something completely up to her. Nagging and prodding only make things worse. You do what you know is right. You be the husband you know she needs. If you need to establish some boundaries in your relationship, then I encourage you to do so. You can love and bless your wife without being a doormat. Maybe your expectations of her are unrealistic. Maybe you need to be clear with her about how such behavior makes you feel; offering something like, "When you _____, it makes me feel _____" (and throw in a mad, sad, glad, or scared). I truly believe that with honest and non-threatening communication, prayer, tenderness, and forgiveness; some changes will begin to take place in your marriage.

---

### Task to Consider:

Tell your wife, "I forgive you for _____." And ask your wife to forgive you for anything you have done to cause her pain (remember these nine words: "I am sorry. I was wrong. Please forgive me.").

# DAY 24 - WORSHIP WITH HER

*"For where two or three are gathered in my name,
I'm there with them"* (Matthew 18:20 CEB).

*"In worship, God imparts himself to us"* (C. S. Lewis).

## Thought for the Day:

Worship is such an important aspect to your life, and to your wife's as well. As the song goes, we were made to worship (women and men alike). Although worship can take numerous forms (serving the homeless, raising faithful children, caring for the Earth, etc.), I want to lift up the value of corporate worship today. What I mean by this is going to a church sanctuary, auditorium, or even tuning in to an online service provided by a local congregation. Some of the benefits that we receive from corporate worship include:

- Worship helps us to remember how God has been so faithful. Deuteronomy 5:15 states, "Remember that you were a slave in Egypt, but the Lord your God brought you out of there with a strong hand and an outstretched arm" (CEB). God has done this for all of us, and we become aware of it as we worship.
- Worship is (for many) an emotional experience, and allows for emotional expression. At White's Chapel (my church home and family), people laugh and cry each and every week. We see people in the midst of great joy, as well as great pain. And the worship that we do together provides an outlet for people to express what they are feeling.
- Worship is so encouraging. It causes us to experience beauty, and so much of what is good in this world (and the next world as well!). It encourages our life, but also our life of faith. Oftentimes we leave worship with our faith batteries recharged and ready to take on another week. In worship we are given the strength to keep going.

- Worship helps us to follow Jesus Christ. Through the singing, reading of scripture, preaching, offering (giving our offering and God's tithe reminds us that everything we have belongs to the Lord, and we are to trust in God - not money), and other elements of worship we come to know and obey God more and more.

- Worship can serve as a reality check for us. Maybe you and your wife have been fighting, or she has been disrespectful towards you, or you've been unkind to her. It is amazing how God can use that hour to impart something that connects with us right where we are (and causes us to rethink our current behavior!).

- Worship is so intimate. It is the holiest of dates. You can sit together. Be in the presence of one another. Hold hands. Be in the presence of God. Live out your faith with a community of believers. I believe there are few things in this world that will bind you and your wife together as one like worship does.

- Worship gives you something positive to talk about. So much of the information we take in is negative and superfluous (a big word meaning "useless"). When you worship with each other, you have a whole week's worth of great stuff to talk about.

- Worship helps you to be grounded, focused, and centered. You are reminded who you are, and whose you are. You are encouraged to be the person you were created to be. You are assured that no matter what comes your way, you have an anchor in your life. You truly are building your home, your marriage, your relationship on rock.

- Worship nourishes and nurtures your soul (and oftentimes your mind as well!).

---

### Task to Consider:

Attend weekly worship at a local congregation (or online) together with your wife.

---

# DAY 25 - HAVE SPIRITUAL CONVERSATIONS WITH HER

*"Look! I'm standing at the door and knocking. If any hear my voice and open the door, I will come in to be with them, and will have dinner with them, and they will have dinner with me"* (Revelation 3:20 CEB).

*"A single conversation across the table with a wise man is better than ten years mere study of books"* (Henry Wadsworth Longfellow).

## Thought for the Day and Several Tasks to Consider:

When I was growing up as a child in rural Northwest Louisiana, I knew that Saturday morning cartoons were over when men wearing camouflage started reeling in big bass (and then letting them go – sustainability at its finest!). We only had three channels on our TV, and those guys (or wrestling) seemed to be on all of them come noon. My brother loved them, and lived for Saturday afternoon fishing shows with Bill Dance and the gang. To tell you the truth, I hated those guys (and to tell you the truth, I love to fish). For some reason, I'm just thinking that your wife (unless she is an avid outdoorswoman) hates that stuff too. She can only take so much of your rambling about ESPN, fantasy football, or God knows what. At some point in time I know she would like to talk with you about something of substance. Now, I'm not saying that you guys need to talk about the kids all the time (you probably already do that), or the house, or vacation, or schedules, or work. What I mean is that it would behoove you to spend some time talking with your wife about some things of eternal value and significance.

Two things that will provide lots of spiritual conversation between the two of you are to worship together regularly (like we talked about yesterday) and to read through and/or study the Bible together. When reading a particular passage from the Bible, ask one another, "What does this passage say about God? What does it say about humankind? What does it say about God's relationship with humankind? What does it say to you?" Having spiritual conversations is not about acquiring information or being spiritually arrogant. It's about you both following Jesus and being discipled, together. Here are a few spiritual conversation starters:

- What is your personal story of coming to faith in Jesus Christ?
- What does Jesus mean to you today?
- What spiritual goals do you have?
- How have you experienced God's blessing in the last week?
- How do you feel the Holy Spirit working in your life, our marriage, our home?
- In what do you ultimately trust?
- Where or when do you see God showing up in your life?
- What values, morals, and ethics are important to you?
- Would you say we have a "Christian" marriage? What does one look like?
- Do our priorities in life align with the faith we profess?
- How would you like to grow spiritually?
- What do you believe about heaven, hell, and the afterlife?
- What is your favorite Bible story, and why?
- What do you feel God calling you to do at this point in your life? How can I help?
- How can we as a married couple change the world for the better?
- When have you felt closest to God? What makes you feel close to God?
- Who are your spiritual heroes?

# DAY 26 - HELP HER GET ENOUGH REST

*"Remember the Sabbath day and treat it as holy"* (Exodus 20:8 CEB).

*"When I die, I want to die like my grandfather who died peacefully in his sleep. Not screaming like all the passengers in his car"* (Will Rogers).

## Thought for the Day:

Is your wife getting enough rest? Is this something with which you could help her? Rest is a spiritual issue not just because it is requested of us by God in the Ten Commandments, but the consequences of not getting enough rest affect us (and our marriage) tremendously. When we don't get enough rest; we become irritable, forgetful, unfocused, fatigued, are more prone to sickness (including increased heart disease), and are even at a higher risk of having an accident. On the flip side, getting enough rest has enormous benefits, including:

- A healthier heart.
- A longer, healthier life.
- Rejuvenates your body.
- Helps control your weight.
- Sparks creativity.
- Focuses your thinking.
- Sharpens your memory.
- Increases your attention.
- Improves physical performance.
- Lowers your stress and potential for depression.
- Increases your alertness and productivity.
- Slows down aging. "Beauty sleep" is not just a fairy tale!
- Increases your overall well-being.

We are encouraged in scripture to replace wearing ourselves out through working too hard by trusting in God. God has given us the Sabbath, a day of rest. In our busy lives today I know very few people who actually take a whole day to rest (whether that be Saturday, Sunday, or another day). So our challenge is to find some blocks of time throughout the week where we can get some rest. And please understand, rest does not necessarily mean sleep.

Meredith rests by reading a book or watching a show. She also requires more sleep than I do, and it behooves me to help her get that full night's rest (or suffer her wrath!). There have been times in our marriage when her need to sleep (including naps) or rest in other ways would get under my skin (so I would complain and be cross with her - great strategy, Bell!). Today I acknowledge her need for rest and down time. I realize what it does for her when I take our children and give her some "quiet" time to do whatever she wants or needs to do (or give her a whole weekend to spend with her girlfriends or family). She is healthier, our marriage is better, when she gets enough rest.

---

### Task to Consider:
Create time for your wife to take a nap or rest is some other way.

---

# DAY 27 - TRUST HER

*"Trust in the Lord with all your heart And do not lean on your own understanding. In all your ways acknowledge Him, And He will make your paths straight"* (Proverbs 3:5, 6 NASB),

*"Many marriages would be better if the husband and the wife clearly understood that they are on the same side"* (Zig Ziglar).

## Thought for the Day:

Do you get angry with your wife? Does she do things that frustrate you, or even just tick you off? Does she sometimes behave in such a way that makes you wonder, "What is she thinking?" My friend, give her the benefit of the doubt. She's not you. She'll never be you. And you don't want her to be you. Give her the benefit of the doubt. Trust her. Before you throw the book at her, give her the verdict of "not guilty." Stop judging her actions and intentions as bad, incorrect, impure, or just plain crazy.

Henry Ford said, "If there is any great secret of success in life, it lies in the ability to put yourself in the other person's place and to see things from his point of view - as well as your own." One great way to cherish your wife is to do this very thing. Instead of practicing criticism (and the nagging that follows - which beats your wife to a pulp), practice understanding. Put yourself in her shoes. Walk a mile in her shoes. Seek to understand who she is, what she does, and why. Take the focus off of yourself, and focus on her. Your marriage isn't just about you, it's about both of you. And one way to love your wife is to trust that who she is and what she does is good, holy, and beautiful.

Now, I'm not asking you to be a gullible doormat. There are issues that come up in marriage that can end it (and these aren't just things men do), such as: affairs, abuse, and addictions. That's not what I'm talking about here. What I'm talking about are those normal everyday things your wife does that just get under your skin. Some of it needs to be addressed, and some of it doesn't. Not every hill is Calvary, and at the end of the day you want your wife to feel loved (believe me, it WILL make a difference in your marriage if you will just STOP judging, critiquing, and criticizing her). Trust her.

Shortly before his crucifixion, Jesus spoke the following words to his closest friends, "Don't be troubled. Trust in God. Trust also in me. My Father's house has room to spare. If that weren't the case, would I have told you that I'm going to prepare a place for you? When I go to prepare a place for you, I will return and take you to be with me so that where I am you will be too" (John 14:1-3 CEB). These must have been such comforting words to the apostles, to know that they had an eternal home with Jesus in Heaven. A place of peace, security, and love; forever. Jesus says, "Trust in God. Trust also in me." Can you say that to your wife? Trust in God, and trust in me. I'm going to make myself a person who is trustworthy, and I'm going to trust you. I'm going to create a home for you, with you, that is peaceful, secure, and loving. Right here. Right now. And for all the years that God gives us together. Jesus promised it to his closest friends. Can you promise it to your closest friend? I pray you will.

---

### Task to Consider:

Give your wife the benefit of the doubt.

---

# DAY 28 - LOVE HER AS CHRIST LOVED THE CHURCH

*"Now faith, hope, and love remain—these three things—and the greatest of these is love"* (1 Corinthians 13:13 CEB).

*"I have learned that only two things are necessary to keep one's wife happy. First, let her think she's having her own way. And second, let her have it"* (Lyndon B. Johnson).

## Thought for the Day:

Matthew, Mark, and Luke all tell us plainly the kind of love Jesus had for those he came to save. Matthew records, "As Jesus was going up to Jerusalem, he took the Twelve aside by themselves on the road. He told them, 'Look, we are going up to Jerusalem. The [Son of Man] will be handed over to the chief priests and legal experts. They will condemn him to death. They will hand him over to the Gentiles to be ridiculed, tortured, and crucified'" (Matthew 20:17-19 CEB). That's a picture of true, genuine, unconditional, with no strings attached love. John reminds us that "God so loved the world that he gave his only Son, so that everyone who believes in him won't perish but will have eternal life" (John 3:16 CEB). However, this passage from Matthew shows us the extent of that love. Jesus loved us so much that he allowed himself to be betrayed, condemned, mocked, tortured, and crucified. He gave everything. He was 100% invested. He withheld nothing. This is total abandon. Everything was on the line, for love.

And Paul tells us to love our wives in a similar fashion. He states, "As for husbands, love your wives just like Christ loved the church and gave himself for her" (Ephesians 5:25 CEB). Wow! Can you do that? I know I can't! Can you put that much faith in your wife? Probably not, but you can put that much faith in God. Is your wife big enough (pardon the expression) to give you reason to put that kind of hope in her? Probably not, but God is big enough. Are you willing to put everything on the line, for love? For her?

At this season in your marriage, this might be too big of a thing to ask (and that's OK). Maybe where we need to start is much much simpler. Maybe what you need to do is show your wife you love her in some small way. Just do one little thing today that lets her know you are thinking about her, and that she's a blip on your radar. Don't worry about tomorrow or next week (or her birthday!). Just think about one tiny thing you can do today. Maybe out of the blue you can tell her, "I love you." Maybe you can give her a random hug. Perhaps you can text her something sweet. Maybe you can call her and ask her if you can pick up anything from the store on your way home. Maybe you can fix her a cup of coffee and take it to her. How about telling her she looks pretty? What if you picked out a card for her, signed it, and left it somewhere for her to find? Maybe you take the kids for ice cream and give her an hour of quiet. Maybe you can just buy her some chocolate, a magazine, or something small that she enjoys. These all take very little time, energy, and money; but they'll mean so much to your wife. You don't have to start out by hanging yourself on a cross to prove your love toward her. Just tell her and show her each and every day in some small way that she is the love of your life.

If you're married, and you love your wife, is it enough to only tell her you love her on your wedding day? Of course not! She needs to hear this and receive this from you every single day.

---

### Task to Consider:

Decide on one small way to show your wife you love her today, and do it.

---

# CONCLUSION

*"Love is patient, love is kind and is not jealous; love does not brag and is not arrogant, does not act unbecomingly; it does not seek its own, is not provoked, does not take into account a wrong suffered, does not rejoice in unrighteousness, but rejoices with the truth; bears all things, believes all things, hopes all things, endures all things"*
(1 Corinthians 13:4-7 NASB).

I gotta say, man, I'm proud of you. You have stuck with this. You've read a bunch of stuff that may or may not have made much sense (which is much more of a comment about the author than your intelligence). You've stretched yourself, and it's my great hope that your wife has felt blessed because of your effort (and that your marriage has gotten even better).

Although this book has primarily been about focusing on your wife, I must say that the personal benefits for you of making her feel loved are numerous. Sean Russell is an amazing singer/songwriter who lives in my neighborhood. His song, *Rabbits* (which shares how his life is greatly affected by the presence and love of his wife), captures some of this wisdom. Sean writes, "She sees the world in a way that I've forgotten or ignored. She sees the man that I don't see."[6] When you live with a wife who feels blessed, then you, my friend, will be a blessed man (and as Sean writes, your soul will shine). Marriage is one of the greatest and primary vehicles God uses to form men spiritually[7] (which might be the reason why so

---

6   www.seanrussellmusic.com/.

7   Gary Thomas lifts this concept up beautifully and powerfully in his book, *Sacred Marriage*.

many men allow their marriage to exist in a state of misery – it keeps us in control so this can't happen)!

As you continue to live this new life with your wife, here are a few things to keep in mind. Blessing your wife is not about manipulation. If your blessing is fueled by ulterior motives and agendas, then it won't be much of a blessing at all. Intentionally loving on your wife is not about getting her in bed (although that has been known to happen at times!). Your motive is to bless her, with no strings attached.

The kind of love we've been talking about in this book is tenacious. It has grit. It looks to the present and future with a stubborn and determined resolve to keep going. The Energizer Bunny has nothing on this kind of unconditional love. Batteries stop working. In fact, everything that is of this world eventually stops, breaks down, degrades, and ceases to exist. But not love. Not real love. Not Godly love that comes with no strings attached. This love cannot be rocked by the challenges of life and human relationships. This love that holds one close when they need to be held close, and lets them go when they need to be let go, just won't stop. The love that Jesus taught us to give is like a Sharpie. It is permanent. Once you've made a mark, there is no going back. There is no erasing it. Scrub as much as you want, but it's still there. This love "puts up with anything, trusts God always, always looks for the best, never looks back, but keeps going to the end" (1 Corinthians 13:7 MSG). This love claims you can hang Jesus on a cross and bury him in the ground, but he will rise. He will always rise. Because his love never ends. It never fails.

I pray the same for you, and the love you have for your wife. She needs you. She loves you. You are the man of her dreams. So go make her dreams come true. God bless you, now go bless your wife!

# AFTERWORD

Steven mentioned to me one day that he was writing a book. I shared how I thought that was a great idea. I noticed that he had been up late at his "desk" in our home, which is our dining room table. Seeing him there reminded me of when he was writing his dissertation into the early-morning hours for months and months. Because I am often caught up in the pace of our life, I had failed to ask him more about his book, such as the title and the subject. Finally, at least three months into his work, I paused long enough to learn more. I was speechless when he told me that his book was about husbands blessing their wives. Could it be true that my husband was passionate enough about making our marriage work that he would take the time to write a book about it? It is true, and our marriage continues to grow stronger because of his commitment.

There are many relationships that we have in our lives, and many people we see on a day-to-day basis. These relationships help, heal, encourage, inspire, and sometimes hurt us along our journey through life. There is one relationship that is more important than any other relationship that you have with the people in your life. That relationship is the one you have with your wife. She, unlike others, has promised before God that she will walk with you through her entire life to love, support, honor, heal, and keep you. She made a promise to build a life with you, and to fill your home with memories. She made a promise to love you on your good days, and on your dark days. Even if she does not remind you of her promise each day, it is there under the surface, I promise.

By simply reading these devotionals, you are giving a gift to your wife. Taking it a step further is a blessing to your wife that reminds her that your promise is still alive too. The notes I find by my sink in the morning on bits of paper, the chocolate bar handed to me after a trip to the store, the date that I suddenly find myself on with Steven, are all ways that show me that his promise to me is still alive. I am sure you know how to bless your wife. I hope you are now motivated to focus on your wife and bless her. After all, you are her number-one person on this journey of life too.

Rev. Meredith Bell
Pastor for Women's Ministry, White's Chapel United Methodist Church

Made in the USA
Charleston, SC
21 May 2014